T0196153

ABOUT YOU

ELIZABETH PIPKO

ARCHWAY
PUBLISHING

Archway Publishing books may be ordered through booksellers or by contacting:

Archway Publishing
1663 Liberty Drive
Bloomington, IN 47403
www.archwaypublishing.com
1 (888) 242-5904

ISBN: 978-1-4808-6310-1 (sc)
ISBN: 978-1-4808-6309-5 (e)

Library of Congress Control Number: 2018905798

Print information available on the last page.

Archway Publishing rev. date: 05/14/2018

For Darren,

I'll love you forever

And in loving memory of Dedushka Markusha.

The world is nothing without you

"Elizabeth Pipko's new poetry collection, About You, delicately traces the arcs and loops of young love upon the ice of heartache. Pipko's poems stammer through the blizzard of their own making, attended by the angels of a sensitive and perceptive nature. These are perfect poems for teenagers looking into the snow globe of young adulthood with all of its difficult weathers of desire, lust, pain, and loss. If you have ever had your heart broken, if you have ever burned for someone just out of reach and forever retreating from you, you will find comfort and strength in the pages of About You."

- Dante Di Stefano, Author of the 2017 Paterson poetry prize honor book, Love Is a Stone Endlessly in Flight

Contents

You 1

The More Things Change 3

December 5

Disappear 7

Mine 9

Free 11

Choosing You 13

Puppeteer 15

When You Took My Hand 17

Go Ahead 19

Favorite Sweater 21

Stuck 23

All Right 25

Tonight 27

Fate 29

Me 31

Pretend 33

Today 35

Why? 37

It Wasn't You 39

All a Waste 41

Long Ago 43

Finally 45

If Only I Had Known 47

You

What about seeing the world?
What about our plans?
What happened to being safe
In each other's hands?

Where did our dreams go?
What about being together?
Don't you remember looking at me
And whispering, "forever"?'

Where do I turn?
This isn't fair
You said you'd love me
You said you'd be there

What about your promises?
What about my surprise?
Don't you ever miss
Looking into each other's eyes?

Now what?
What am I to do?
It was never him
It was always you

The More Things Change

When the leaves have turned to brown
And the sky has turned to gray
When the birds have hatched
And the rain has dried away

When the sea has kissed the shore
And the icicles have dried
When the sun has set
And all the tears have been cried

When the year has passed us by
And December's turned to June
When the stars have reappeared
Just to circle 'round the moon

I'll look down at my notebook
And I'll see your name
Because the more things change
The more they stay the same

December

Your hand in mine
Our long walks in the park
Your whispers in the movies
Our kisses in the dark

My hand on your chest
The snowflakes in our hair
Our cotton blanket
The creaky rocking chair

The bumpy carriage rides
My favorite long-stemmed rose
Our frozen fingers
The icicles on my nose

Our snowball fights
On that lazy afternoon
Sipping hot chocolate
How we sat and watched the moon

Do me one favor
Kiss me please before you go
It'll keep me warm
As I stammer through the snow

Disappear

Her skin was luscious, peachy clean
Her eyes a chocolate brown
Her smile full of life
The envy of her town

She walked with angels on each side
Her hair flowing in the wind
Curls hanging down like waterfalls
Her dress so neatly pinned

Men watched as she would walk on by
Giving everyone a glare
Heads would turn, and all would yearn
Stopping just to stare

She skipped along so gracefully
You would think she had no fear
But with each step she'd close her eyes
And pray to disappear

Mine

I'll meet you in a field of green
Air so crisp and sky so blue
Or maybe in a rainforest
With waterfalls and fresh bamboo

I'll hold your hand and squeeze it tight
Never letting go
I'll share my thoughts, all through the night
Praying for the clock to slow

I'll laugh and dance around for you
While you look on
My dress flailing in the wind
A scene of white chiffon

We'll sit around and watch the sun
As it sets behind the trees
We'll watch the ants begin to run
As they feel the water's breeze

The moon will take over
As the stars begin to shine
I'll fall asleep to the thought
Of one day calling you mine

Free

If you love me won't you let me know?
Before I'm old and gray

If you love me, please don't let me go
I beg of you, please stay

If you love me, hold my hand,
Breathe me in and squeeze me tight

If you love me won't you hold me close
All throughout the night?

If you love me won't you kiss my lips,
run your fingers through my hair
If you love me prove it; if you love me, swear

If you love me look into my eyes
Tell me what you see

If you love her take this life of mine
I'll finally be free

Choosing You

You can ask me in the morning
You can ask me in the night
You can scare me in the darkness
Or come running when it's bright
Come and find me when I'm lonely
Or when I'm bouncing 'round with glee
Interrupt me when I'm busy
Or wake me up at three
Ask me when it's raining
Ask me when the sky is blue
I'd be lying if I said I wouldn't go on choosing you

Puppeteer

I'm not awake without you
The days just float on by

I'm not alive without you
Haven't lived since we said goodbye

I can't breathe without you
Knowing that you're not around

I can't live without you
The day you left, I drowned

I can't see without you
Nothing looks the way it should

I can't hear without you
Everything's misunderstood

There's no point in life without you
There's no life if you're not here

I'm simply lost without you
You're my puppeteer

When You Took

My Hand

Matthew wrote me poems
Robert kissed me in the rain

Daniel showered me with presents
John took me straight to Spain

Andrew sent three dozen roses
Douglas never let me go

Alan took me to the theater
Josh carried me through the snow

James took me to fancy restaurants
Billy sang the sweetest tune

Alex bought me diamonds
With Seth I sat and watched the moon

Max took me on a sleigh ride
Joel built me castles in the sand

But none of that compared
To when you took my hand

Go Ahead

If the world would turn to dust
And all of life would disappear

My love for you would turn to lust
My hope for us would turn to fear

If my dreams would fall apart
And you'd leave my side

I'd have but an empty heart
To forever match my pride

The sun would set before it should
The stars would hide away

The moon would crumble as it could
The sky would turn to gray

If I awaken to the sound
Of an empty room

Go ahead and dig the ground
I'll make this place my tomb

Favorite Sweater

You're old, you're small
You're not the same
Your threads have turned to mold

And yet the remembrance of your name
Means more to me than gold

You've shrunken in too many ways
Your length just isn't right

Just the feeling of your touch
Reminds me all too well of that night

You make me think of better days
We used to fit like bread and butter

And now your presence isn't right
You're just adding to the clutter

It's over now, all set and done
it's all in the past

Love, I've now been forced to learn
Like my favorite sweater, couldn't last

Stuck

We've made quite a mess my friend
Just look at the ground

What have we done my friend?
All these pieces thrown around

We started with a diamond
We're left with quite a spill

Was it worth the pain my friend?
Was it worth the thrill?

I think we've destroyed it
Everything is gone I fear

I think we're out of time
Everything's ruined my dear

Not all fairytales work out my friend
I wish we could start anew

Should've stopped this sooner
Now I'm stuck in love with you

All Right

It may have been the shining lights
It may have been the sounds

Perhaps the scene around us
In that vacant gloomy town

Maybe it was the lyrics
Being pounded through our ears

Or possibly the thought
That we're almost out of years

It could've been the moon
Staring down at us, so bright

Giving us something to share
On that dark and frozen night

Or maybe it was your hand
Holding on to mine so tight

Maybe it was having you
That made it all, all right

Tonight

He doesn't have your wit
He doesn't have your skills
He doesn't give me shivers
He doesn't give me chills
His eyes don't sparkle
His smile doesn't shine
His arms don't fit around me
His jokes are not divine
His humor makes no sense to me
His laugh, it isn't rare
His thoughts aren't exciting
His charm doesn't compare
He doesn't make me wonder
About him I don't dream
He isn't in my thoughts
In my mind he doesn't gleam
Maybe we're not meant to be
Maybe we're not right
But at least I know
He'll stay by my side tonight

Fate

Blood like a stone
From the edge of my skate
Tears through my heart
Like the sharp pain of hate

Your words have wrecked me
Your job is done
You can go now
You've finally won

Your spirit is evil
On a whole different level
Words can't describe you
You're simply the devil

Your actions are troubling
Your thoughts, a disgrace
Your wicked glare
Consumes your whole face

You've left me alone
With just one final breath
Nobody told me
This love would end in death

Blood like a stone
From the edge of my skate
Wish I had known
This would be our fate

Me

I miss your face
I miss your hands
I miss touching your hair

I miss your eyes
I miss your curls
I miss your loving stare

I miss your voice
I miss your laugh
I miss your gentle stroke

I miss your love
I miss your words
I miss your morning jokes

You turned my life around
In ways I still don't see
There's no one I miss more than you
Except for maybe me

Pretend

I say I'm cold but what I mean
Is that I'm cold inside

When I say I'm empty
I'm only referring to my pride

When I say that I feel torn
I mean torn apart

When I say I'm missing something
I'm referring to my heart

When I imply I'm sad
I don't just mean these tears

I'm referencing the pain
Of living all these years

And when I say I need something
I simply mean a friend

Don't lie and say that's what you are
I hate to pretend

Today

I would have kissed you that much harder
Would have touched you that much more
Would have felt you that much longer
Never would have closed that door

I would have held you that much tighter
Would have let you feel my heart
Would have made you hold me stronger
If I had known we'd one day part

I would have pulled you that much closer
Kept our hands forever tied
'Least I'd know I had you once
'Least I'd know I tried

I would have held you close to me
I would have made you stay
I'd hold on forever more
If you were here today

Why?

Why should I stop the tears from falling
The screams from being heard
Nobody listens anyway
Nobody hears a word

Why should I end the pain
When it hurts so good
Nobody wants to stop it
Nobody thinks they should

Why should I stop the envy
The ache of wanting more
When everyone's out winning
I'm stuck where I was before

Why should I go searching
For the love you think I lack
When everyone's so quick
To stab me in the back

Don't tell me to be happy
I hate to pretend
You're the one that told me
All good things must come to an end

It Wasn't You

My thoughts have taken over
I can no longer feel
I don't know what's left of me
I don't know if I can heal

These visions keep replaying
I close my eyes and see your face
It's your name that I've been saying
In this world I can't erase

I see you everywhere I look
The green grass, the sky so blue
And I'm forced to ask myself
Am I really seeing you?

You're different when I hear your voice
You're different when you're here
Only in my mind I think
Is everything so clear

It wasn't you that I was seeing
You were just inside my head
I fear that that you, has no being
I think that you, has long been dead

All a Waste

If only we could turn back time
Wipe our tears and drift away
If only we could tell ourselves
What we have is here to stay

Some things are indescribable
They all come as a surprise
Like growing up, growing old
Or getting lost deep in your eyes

Sometimes you meet somebody
Who changes what you see
Suddenly you're not missing him
You're missing 'you and me'

We lost our spark, we lost our flame
Somewhere in all the haste
How sad when you can tell yourself
This love was all a waste

Long Ago

I'm not what you want
I'm not what you need
I can't smile, I can't laugh
I can only bleed

I'm not right for you
I'll only bring you down
Don't hang on to me
I can only drown

Trust me, there's no use
Just leave me on the floor
I've gotten what I need
There's no need for more

Leave me where you found me
That's where I belong
You think I'm what you need
But you couldn't be more wrong

You think that you want me
But there's something you should know
I'm nothing short of worthless
I was shattered much too long ago

Finally

Chained up like a prisoner
All my life I had no hopes
Finally, I've saved myself
Finally, I've cut the ropes

I've torn apart your shackles
I walk all on my own
I'm done following your steps
I'm done being your clone

Now I have my chance
To show this world my might
My time has come
I can see the light

I've waited for this moment
Lord knows how much I prayed
I can do this on my own
I no longer need your aid

Finally, I've found the strength
To burst from my cocoon
Too bad this came so late
Too bad I'll die so soon

If Only I

Had Known

I feel it in my veins,
I feel it in my hair
I feel it in my breath,
when I see you standing there

I'm not scared to look you in the eyes
I'm not scared of all you know
The scars you think you've left
Have healed too long ago

I was trapped inside myself
All these powers were my own
All this time I blamed your face
If only I had known

The tunnel may be closing in
But I can see the light
Who knows what I'm capable of?
I've just begun my fight

Printed in the United States
By Bookmasters